The Best Pet for Me

Is a TURTLE a Good Pet for Me?

Therese M. Shea

PowerKiDS press

New York

Published in 2020 by The Rosen Publishing Group, Inc.
29 East 21st Street, New York, NY 10010

First Edition

Editor: Elizabeth Krajnik
Book Design: Rachel Rising

Photo Credits: Cover, p.1 Baishev/Shutterstock.com; Back cover, p. 3 KITSANANAN/Shutterstock.com; Cover, 1, 3, 4, 6, 8,10,12,14,16,18, 20, 22, 23, 24 (background) Anna_leni/Shutterstock.com; p. 4 Mr. SUTTIPON YAKHAM/ Shutterstock.com; p. 5 Amanda Nicholls/Shutterstock.com; p. 6 Bayanova Svetlana/ Shutterstock.com; pp. 7 (yellow-bellied slider), 10 Eric Isselee/Shutterstock.com; p. 7 (red-eared slider) Lepas/Shutterstock.com; p. 7 (Russian tortoise) Susan Schmitz/ Shutterstock.com; p. 7 (West African sideneck turtles) fivespots/Shutterstock.com; p. 7 (western painted turtle) phugunfire/Shutterstock.com; p. 7 (Greek tortoise) arka38/Shutterstock.com; p. 8 cynoclub/Shutterstock.com; p. 9 ET1972/ Shutterstock.com; p. 11 goffredo iacobino/Shutterstock.com; p. 12 Kues/Shutterstock. com; p. 13 GeorgiaCowgirl/Shutterstock.com; p. 14 Africa Studio/Shutterstock.com; p. 15 Dmitry Naumov/Shutterstock.com; p. 16 Mendelex/Shutterstock.com; p. 17 La India Piaroa/Shutterstock.com; p. 18 Samuel Borges Photography/ Shutterstock.com; p. 19 Kristina Ethridge/Shutterstock.com; p. 20 Vikulin/Shutterstock. com; p. 21 imagenavi/Getty Images.

Library of Congress Cataloging-in-Publication Data

Names: Shea, Therese M., author.
Title: Is a turtle a good pet for me? / Therese M. Shea.
Description: New York : PowerKids Press, [2020] | Series: The best pet for me | Includes index.
Identifiers: LCCN 2018053191| ISBN 9781725301207 (paperback) | ISBN 9781725301221 (library bound) | ISBN 9781725301214 (6 pack)
Subjects: LCSH: Turtles as pets–Juvenile literature.
Classification: LCC SF459.T8 S54 2020 | DDC 639.3/924–dc23
LC record available at https://lccn.loc.gov/2018053191

Manufactured in the United States of America

CPSIA Compliance Information: Batch #CSPK19. For Further Information contact Rosen Publishing, New York, New York at 1-800-237-9932.

Contents

Time for a Turtle?

Have you ever thought about getting a pet turtle? Turtles are **reptiles** that have a body inside a bony shell. There are more than 250 species, or kinds, of turtles. They live in many different **habitats**, including deserts, forests, ponds, and oceans. They live on every **continent** except Antarctica. Amazingly, turtles have survived on Earth for about 200 million years!

Many people think turtles are easy to care for. However, they need a lot of special care and plenty of space to grow. Turtles can live for many years and are therefore a big **commitment**. Is a turtle the best pet for you?

Pet Report

A tortoise is a member of the turtle family Testudinidae. All tortoises live only on land. However, not all land-**dwelling** turtles are tortoises. Tortoises live on all continents except Antarctica and Australia.

Turtles can be many sizes. The leatherback turtle (shown below) is more than 6 feet (1.8 m) long. The speckled tortoise is less than 4 inches (10.2 cm) long.

Choose a Turtle

Of the many kinds of turtles, only a few make good pets. It's impossible for many kinds of turtles to live in your home. For example, sea turtles need to live in the ocean, and the giant tortoises of the Galápagos Islands are over 3 feet (0.9 m) long. But some kinds of turtles make great pets.

The first step in becoming a turtle owner is deciding whether you'd like a land-dwelling turtle or a water-dwelling turtle. Both kinds are sold in pet stores. However, if possible, you should adopt your turtle from a local animal shelter or rescue group.

Pet Report

Terrapins are turtles that spend less time in the water than other turtles. They live near bodies of brackish water, or water that is a mixture of salty and fresh. However, this term is usually only used to refer to the diamondback terrapin.

These are just a few of the turtles you can get as a pet. You can **research** other kinds of turtles, too. Water-dwelling turtles can cost less than $20. Land-dwelling turtles often cost more than that.

Possible Pet Turtles

Yellow-Bellied Slider
5 to 12 inches (12.7 to 30.5 cm)
Mostly water dwelling

Red-Eared Slider
8 to 10 inches (20.3 to 25.4 cm)
Mostly water dwelling

Russian Tortoise
6 to 7 inches (15.2 to 17.8 cm)
Land dwelling

African Sideneck Turtle
6 to 9 inches (15.2 to 22.9 cm)
Water dwelling

Western Painted Turtle
7 to 8 inches (17.8 to 20.3 cm)
Water dwelling

Greek Tortoise
6 to 10 inches (15.2 to 25.4 cm)
Land dwelling

Your Turtle's Home

A water-dwelling turtle needs a large aquarium. The turtle needs water to swim in. However, it also needs a dry area to climb on, such as a rock or a stand. Turtles need to bask, or lie in a warm place, out of the water.

A land-dwelling turtle needs a **terrarium** lined with bedding such as soil, bark, or sand. You'll also need a water bowl for the turtle to drink from and splash in. Land-dwelling turtles also need a place to bask and a place to hide.

Turtles need light and heat in their tanks. You'll need special lights and two **thermometers** to check temperatures.

Pet Report

In most turtle aquariums, the water should be about 78°Fahrenheit (26°Celsius). The basking area should be about 85°Fahrenheit (29°Celsius). In a terrarium, the basking side should be about 95°Fahrenheit (35°Celsius). The other side should be about 75°Fahrenheit (24°Celsius). Temperatures should be cooler at night.

Turtles need 12 hours of light each day to keep their bones and shells healthy, but their tank shouldn't be in direct sunlight. You'll need a special light that acts as the sun and another light for basking.

Clean Water

A pet water-dwelling turtle depends on its owner to clean its water. Your water-dwelling turtle will need a **filter** in its tank to help take waste out of the water. However, you'll still need to change your turtle's water every week or two depending on the size of the tank.

Land-dwelling turtles need the water in their bowl changed at least once a day. Different kinds of turtles, both land dwelling and water dwelling, need different levels of humidity, or water in the air. To control the tank's humidity, you may need to buy a machine called a humidifier. You should keep track of the tank's humidity with a tool called a hygrometer.

Pet Report

One way to make sure your turtle stays healthy is keeping its water clean. You should plan on spending a few hours every week caring for your turtle and its home.

It's important to take out uneaten food because it can make your turtle's aquarium or terrarium dirty faster. Some people feed their turtles in a separate tank.

Your Turtle's Diet

Your turtle's diet, or what it eats, is important. A turtle can get sick if it doesn't get enough of the right **nutrients**. Some species of turtles are herbivores, which means they only eat plants. Land-dwelling turtles eat mostly fresh vegetables, such as kale, sweet potatoes, and bell peppers, and some fruits, such as apples and grapes. You may also need to add **supplements** to your turtle's diet.

Other species of turtles are omnivores, which means they eat meat and plants. Some turtles may like crickets, mealworms, comet goldfish, and other small animals. You can also give your turtle special **pellets** or canned food and green leafy vegetables.

You should check with a vet to find out the best foods for your turtle. You can also ask them how much and how often to feed your turtle.

Get to Know Your Turtle

Some turtles are more **social** than others. Some may hide a lot. Some turtles may swim to the surface of the water or walk toward the glass to say "hello." You should only touch your turtle when you have to. If you need to pick it up, use both hands to hold both sides of its shell. Be careful. Your turtle may kick and try to scratch or even bite.

Over time, you'll get to know your turtle's likes and dislikes. It may like to be pet on its head or shell, or even under its chin. You can also train your turtle to eat from your hand.

Pet Report

Some people choose to let their tortoises walk outside when the weather's nice. If you choose to do this with your tortoise, be sure to keep it in a safe place away from other animals.

Keep a good grip on your turtle when you hold it. If you don't, it may fall out of your hands and get hurt.

Sick Turtles

Just like all animals, your turtle may get sick. For example, turtles that don't get enough vitamin A may not eat, lack energy, or have breathing problems. Some turtles get abscesses, which are hard, swollen areas in the body.

Harmful bacteria can cause breathing problems in turtles. A turtle that has breathing problems may stretch its neck out with each breath or may breathe through its mouth.

Turtles can have tiny harmful organisms, such as roundworms, in their body that cause them to lose weight. If you think your turtle isn't looking or acting normally, you should take it to a vet.

Pet Report

Turtles can have problems with their shell. Bacteria or **fungi** can cause a condition called shell rot. Turtle shells can also fracture, or break.

If your turtle gets sick, a vet can run tests to see what's wrong. Your turtle may need different food or special medicine to make it better.

Danger!

You might be surprised to learn that pet turtles can be dangerous—and even deadly. Some turtles may carry bacteria called *Salmonella* on their shells and skin. This kind of bacteria is harmless to the turtle but can make people very sick. Some people can even die. Babies, young children, and older people need to be careful around turtles.

There's no way to tell if a turtle has *Salmonella* just by looking at it. That's why it's very important to wash your hands with soap and water after handling any turtle. All surfaces the turtle touches should be cleaned thoroughly, too.

Pet Report

In the United States, it's against the law to buy or sell a turtle with a shell less than 4 inches (10.2 cm) long. This law was put in place in 1975 to keep children from getting *Salmonella* poisoning.

The Centers for Disease Control and Prevention (CDC) suggests that people with children younger than five years old shouldn't have pet turtles.

The Right Fit for You?

Before you decide if you want a pet turtle, think about whether you're ready for the **responsibility**. Remember, you'll be in charge of feeding it, cleaning its tank, and keeping it healthy. You'll need money for buying the turtle and its aquarium or terrarium and taking it to the vet for regular checkups.

Many turtles live at least 20 years or longer! There's more to think about and look up before you decide if a turtle is the best pet for you. But if you do get a turtle, you'll have an interesting companion for years to come.

Are you ready to get a pet turtle? A turtle can be a great pet if you take good care of it!

What You'll Need

For Water-Dwelling Turtle	For Land-Dwelling Turtle
Cost: $5 for red-eared slider	**Cost:** $80 for Russian tortoise
Aquarium: about $150	**Terrarium:** about $150
Screen for aquarium: $30	**Screen for terrarium:** $30
Filter: $70	**Soil, sand, or rocks:** $20
UV and basking light: $50	**UV and basking light:** $50
Water heater: $25	**Humidifier:** $50
Air pump: $15	**Water dish:** $15
Two thermometers: $20	**Two thermometers:** $20
Basking stand: $25	**Rock for basking or hiding:** $15
Food: about $30 per month	**Food:** about $30 per month
First vet visit: about $120	**First vet visit:** about $120
Estimated cost for beginning supplies: $540	**Estimated cost for beginning supplies: $580**

Glossary

commitment: An agreement to do something.

continent: One of the seven great masses of land on Earth.

dwell: To live in a place.

filter: A machine that is used to remove something unwanted from something, such as water, that passes through it.

fungus: A living thing that is like a plant but doesn't have leaves, flowers, or green color, or make its own food. The plural form is fungi.

habitat: The natural home for plants, animals, and other living things.

nutrient: Something taken in by a plant or animal that helps it grow and stay healthy.

pellet: A usually small, rounded piece of food.

reptile: A cold-blooded animal with thin, dry pieces of skin called scales.

research: Careful study that is done to find and report new knowledge about something.

responsibility: The quality or state of being in charge of someone or something.

social: Tending to form relationships with others.

supplement: Something that is added to something else in order to make it complete.

terrarium: A glass or plastic container used for keeping plants or small animals.

thermometer: An instrument, or tool, used for measuring temperature.

Index

Websites

Due to the changing nature of Internet links, PowerKids Press has developed an online list of websites related to the subject of this book. This site is updated regularly. Please use this link to access the list: www.powerkidslinks.com/bpfm/turtle